DATE			

The Life Cycle of a

Dog

by Lisa Trumbauer

Consulting Editor: Gail Saunders-Smith, Ph.D.

Consultant: Ronald L. Rutowski, Professor,
Department of Biology, Arizona State University

Pebble Books

an imprint of Capstone Press
Mankato, Minnesota

Pebble Books are published by Capstone Press
151 Good Counsel Drive, P.O. Box 669, Mankato, Minnesota 56002
http://www.capstone-press.com

1 2 3 4 5 6 07 06 05 04 03 02

Library of Congress Cataloging-in-Publication Data
Trumbauer, Lisa, 1963–
    The life cycle of a dog/by Lisa Trumbauer.
    p. cm.—(Life cycles)
    Includes bibliographical references (p. 23) and index.
    Summary: Simple text and photographs present the life cycle of a dog.
    ISBN 0-7368-1184-2
    1. Dogs—Life cycles—Juvenile literature. [1. Dogs. 2. Animals—Infancy.]
I. Title. II. Life cycles (Mankato, Minn.)
SF426.5 .T78 2002
636.7—dc21   2001003110

Note to Parents and Teachers

The Life Cycles series supports national science standards related to life science. This book describes and illustrates the life cycle of a dog. The photographs support early readers in understanding the text. The repetition of words and phrases helps early readers learn new words. This book also introduces early readers to subject-specific vocabulary words, which are defined in the Words to Know section. Early readers may need assistance to read some words and to use the Table of Contents, Words to Know, Read More, Internet Sites, and Index/Word List sections of the book.

Table of Contents

Photographs in this book show the life cycle of a beagle.

newborn

A dog begins
life as a puppy.

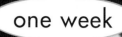
one week

Puppies cannot see or hear when they are born.

8

A mother dog takes care
of her puppies. They drink
milk from her body.

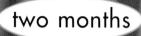two months

10

Puppies grow fast.

Their eyes and ears open.

They sleep, eat, and play.

adult

12

Puppies become adults
in about one year.
Dogs can live
up to 15 years.

A female dog goes into heat two times a year. She attracts a male dog. The two dogs mate.

Puppies grow inside
the female dog
for two months.

The female dog
gives birth to a litter
of puppies. She licks
the puppies clean.

one week

newborn

two months

adult

The puppies are the start of a new life cycle.

Words to Know

adult—an animal that is able to mate; some dogs continue to grow larger after becoming adults; the color of some dogs changes as they grow.

attract—to get the attention of someone or something; when dogs are attracted to each other, they move closer to each other.

heat—the time when a female dog is ready to mate; female dogs go into heat every six months.

life cycle—the stages in the life of an animal; the life cycle includes being born, growing up, having young, and dying.

litter—a group of animals born at the same time to one mother; most dog litters have three to six puppies; female dogs can have two litters each year.

milk—the white liquid produced by the bodies of female mammals

Read More

Dolbear, Emily J., and E. Russell Primm. *Dogs Have Puppies.* Animals and Their Young. Minneapolis: Compass Point Books, 2001.

Powell, Jillian. *From Puppy to Dog.* How Do They Grow? Austin, Texas: Raintree Steck-Vaughn, 2001.

Royston, Angela. *Life Cycle of a Dog.* Chicago: Heinemann Library, 2000.

Internet Sites

AKC Kids' Corner
http://www.akc.org/love/dah/kidskorn/spring01/
akcspring2001/home.html

Beagle
http://www.enchantedlearning.com/subjects/mammals/
dog/beagleprintout.shtml

Fact Monster: Dog
http://klnlive.factmonster.com/ce6/sci/A0815770.html

Index/Word List

Word Count: 110
Early-Intervention Level: 14

Editorial Credits
Sarah Lynn Schuette, editor; Jennifer Schonborn, production designer and interior
  illustrator; Kia Bielke, cover designer; Kimberly Danger and Mary Englar,
  photo researchers

Photo Credits
Jon Blumb, 4, 6, 20 (left, top)
Mark Raycroft, cover, 1, 12, 14, 16, 20 (bottom)
Norvia Behling, 10, 20 (right)
TwainHeart Beagles, 8
www.ronkimball/stock.com, 18

PLEASE SHARE YOUR THOUGHTS
ON THIS BOOK

comments:	comments:
comments:	comments:
comments:	comments:
comments:	comments:
comments:	comments:
comments:	comments: